IMM
Integrated Modeling Method
Information Flow Modeling

11th Edition

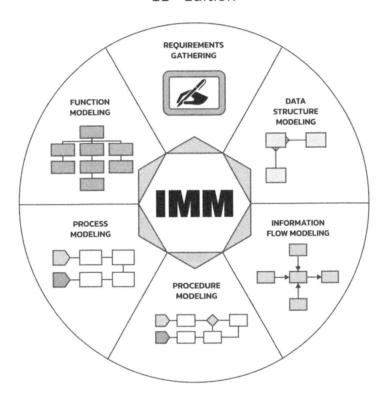

Copyright © Integrated Modeling Method 2023

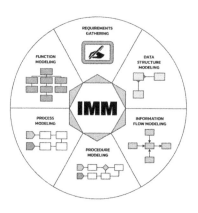

Table of Contents

1.   The Integrated Modeling Method

Introducing the game-changing Integrated Modeling Method (IMM) – a one-of-a-kind approach to business analysis and modeling that transforms the way analysts and business managers unleash the full potential of business improvement and systems development projects in their Enterprise. After years of dedicated development, we're thrilled to unveil the power of IMM on Kindle and Amazon and empower you with the tools to create powerful Business Architecture Models that bring real and tangible business benefits.

IMM stands at the forefront of analysis and modeling innovation, seamlessly blending the best practices from a diverse range of powerful modeling techniques. It's a holistic solution that captures the essence of truly powerful business systems modeling, ensuring you have all the right tools at your fingertips.

IMM's mission is simple yet transformative: to enable the swift production of elegant, accurate, and integrated Architectural Models for your entire Enterprise or for specific segments. With a focus on accuracy and rigor, IMM ensures that you can swiftly navigate the modeling process, while avoiding the limitations and pitfalls of conventional methods.

Say goodbye to complex and time-consuming modeling processes. IMM injects an upbeat and efficient spirit into your projects, allowing you to produce remarkable models with ease. It's the ultimate blend of speed, precision, and integration, so you can focus on what matters most – driving your Enterprise forward.

Using the IMM suite of books you can embrace a future where analysis and modeling is an enjoyable and rewarding experience. Watch as your ideas come to life, backed by the reliability and insights that IMM offers.

1.1. Elements of IMM

IMM provides you with a full suite of powerful modeling techniques, each of which was developed to maximize accuracy, effectiveness and productivity when modeling particular aspects of an Enterprise. All of these are techniques are fully integrated and comprise the following:

Requirements Gathering	The success of all business improvement projects depends on the *quality* and *completeness* of the information you collect during the Requirements Gathering stage. The power of IMM starts with its unique, INTEGRATED approach to Requirements Gathering, which enables you to gather requirements for ALL FACETS of your Enterprise through a *single set of interview questions*.
Business Function Architecture	The Business Function Architecture lies at the heart of every Enterprise and, so, is at the heart of IMM. It is a unique catalogue of the core activities an Enterprise must perform to meet its objectives and continue in existence. These core activities are called Business Functions.

Data Architecture Modeling   This is the technique used to identify and model the elements of data, and the way in which these elements are related to each other, so an *Enterprise* can create the INFORMATION it requires to effectively execute its Business Functions. The *Data Architecture Model* is the cornerstone to success for all *data quality*, *data governance*, *master data management* and *database development* projects.

Business Process Modeling   This is the technique to use when you need to know and model the precise order in which the Business Functions need to be carried out in response to a triggering event and arrive at a predefined and desirable business outcome. For example, "what steps must the Enterprise take, and in what order, to register a new customer and issue their first bill?"

Business Procedure Modeling   This is the technique to use when you need to *know and show* HOW *Business Processes* ought to be implemented on a day-to-day basis using existing technologies and standards.

Information Flow Modeling   This is the technique to use when you need to know and show how information flows into, around and out of the business.

Each of the architecture models in IMM is built based on elements from the Business Function Architecture. Because of this, all the models are fully integrated, which provides a richness, rigor and consistency that is not currently offered by any other business architecture modeling method.

1.2. First Things First

The starting point for all modeling in IMM is the Function Catalogue as it lies at the core of IMM and acts as the unique catalogue of all the Functions that will be used in all other models.

The Function Catalogue does not have to be built in its entirety in advance of other models. However, the more you can do on the Function Catalogue prior to starting other modeling the easier your task will be. But the 'I' in IMM not only stands for 'Integrated' but also for 'Interactive'.

Whatever facet of IMM you are using you will always be interacting with the Function Catalogue. This interaction will not be limited simply to using Functions from it in your models but will include adding to and modifying it.

1.3. Before Starting This Book

There are certain terms and concepts with which you should be familiar before starting this book, these are:

- Business Function
- Leaf Business Function
- Business Function Hierarchy
- Elementary Business Function

Although these terms are defined in the Glossary, if you are not thoroughly familiar with them, then we strongly recommend that you read our book IMM Requirements Gathering and Business Function Modeling, available from Amazon and Kindle in both Paperback and eBook format.

We recommend reading the book for three reasons:

- It explains all these terms in context.

- All Information Flow Models are based on Business Functions so, without fully understanding Business Function modeling, it will be more difficult to build effective Information Flow Models.

- The book covers the interviewing techniques needed to gather the information necessary to do effective Information Flow Modeling.

> **To get our book, IMM Requirements Gathering and Business Function Modeling,**
> **from Amazon or Kindle Simply search for "integrated modeling method".**

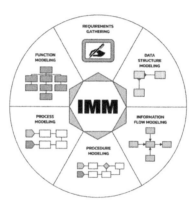

2.   What is a Business Model?

A business model is a means of representing some facet of a business in a way that allows that facet to be better understood, altered, or improved.

There are two major parts to any business model: 1) a diagram pictorially representing a facet of the business and 2) textual descriptions of each of the elements on the diagram. Both parts must exist for the model to be complete. A diagram on its own is not a model!

2.1. Sketch or Diagram?

A sketch diagram is one that contains shapes, lines and text that are supposed to tell a story.

However, what each shape means is not always clear or the same from one diagram to the next. Schematics often only make sense when the person who drew them is there to explain what they mean.

When does a sketch become a diagram?

For a sketch to be classed as a diagram it must show that it uses **standard conventions** and has **rigorous standards**.

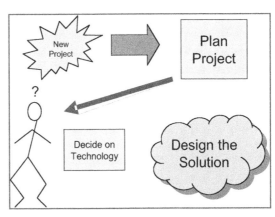

Typical Sketch Diagram

Standard Conventions

The term 'convention' here means 'a way of representing an object on a diagram'. So, a 'standard convention' simply means objects will be represented on diagrams in a consistent manner. For example, a Business Function will not be shown as a circle on a diagram and as a triangle in another place and as a fluffy cloud in yet another!

Rigorous Standards

Rigor is vital in modeling. In its simplest form it means 'always employ the standard conventions', but over and above that, it means to do so in a manner that is **always** the same. Standards will also tell you those things that should appear on a diagrammatic model and those that should not.

2.2. Which Model?

Any model can only represent a part of the item it is trying to model. If we were trying to model the human body we would need to ask, 'what part of the body are we trying to represent?' and then choose the most appropriate modeling technique. If we were trying to model the bone structure, then using a skeleton or an x-ray would both be suitable techniques.

Similarly, in business modeling we must ask the question, 'what facet of the business are we trying to represent?' and then choose the most appropriate modeling technique for that facet. Using the wrong technique can give quite the wrong results, for example, using Information Flow Diagrams to map Business Processes. This is a mistake that has often been made in the past with disastrous results for the businesses concerned.

IMM provides modeling techniques for all facets of a business and, over and above this, enables all the techniques to be integrated through the Business Function Catalogue.

3.   Building Information Flow Models

The following sections describe all the facets of Information Flow Models, when and how to use them and how to avoid errors.

3.1. When to Use Information Flow Models

Information Flow Models (IFM's) are drawn when the business needs to understand how information flows around the business or between the business and the outside world.

When information flows around (inside) the business it flows between Business Functions.

When information flows to and from the outside world it flows between Functions (that are inside the business) and what are called "External Entities". Examples of External Entities are 'Government', 'Supplier', 'Customer', etc.

An Information Flow model consists of two parts:

1.   An Information Flow Diagram (IFD)

2.   Definitions for each element on the IFD

3.2. Elements of an IFD

The following are the only valid elements that can appear on an IFD:

Business Functions	These will be Business Functions from the Function Catalogue.
External Entities	These are entities external to the business, such as Customer, Supplier, etc.
Information Flows	These are the flows of information between Business Functions inside the business or between Business Functions and External Entities.
Title Box	A box with a title text and a descriptive name for the IFD.
Focal Function Box	A rectangle indicating which Function of the diagram is the Focal Function (see Section 3.5 for more details)

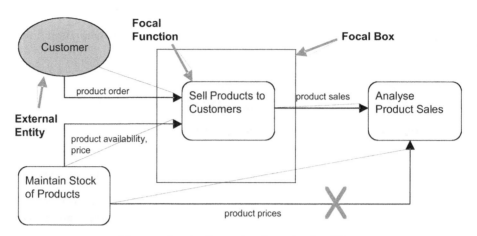

Diagram showing the major elements of an IFD

The Information Flow "product prices" in the diagram above is incorrectly drawn as it is between two Business Functions outside the Focal Box.

3.3. Information Flows

Information flows are shown on the IFD as single headed arrows going between Functions or between Functions and External Entities. These arrows are labelled with the information they represent.

Example of an Information Flow between two Functions

Unlabeled arrows are meaningless and should never appear on an Information Flow diagram.

The Functions that appear on Information Flow diagrams are taken from the **bottom level** of the Function Catalogue as it stands at the present time. Ideally these should be Elementary Business Functions.

3.4. Two Way Information Flow

Double headed arrows should **NOT** be used to show two-way Information Flow as it is not possible to clearly show in which direction each piece of information flows.

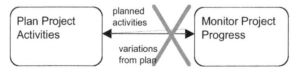

Double headed arrows should NOT be used

Does "planned activities" in the previous diagram flow from left to right or vice versa?

When information flows in two directions between Functions this must be shown by <u>**two**</u> arrows going in **opposite** directions as shown below:

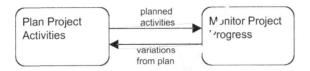

Two-way information flow shown correctly using two arrows

Another reason why a double headed arrow cannot be used is that the content of each information flow needs to be separately defined (see Section 4) and this would not be possible using a single, double headed arrow.

3.5. The Focal Function and Focal Box

The most effective way to build Information Flow Diagrams is to use them to show all the information that flows into and out of **ONE** specific Function. This is called the 'focal Function' and should be placed at the center of the diagram with all other Functions arranged around it.

A square should be drawn around the focal Function. This is called the 'focal box'. The purposes of the focal box are 1) to clearly show which is the focal Function and 2) to keep the diagram as uncluttered as possible by following these simple rules:

- Information flows should not be drawn between two items if they are both outside the focal box.
- When an item is inside the focal box then **ALL** information flows to and from it **MUST** be shown on the diagram.
- External entities must always be outside the focal box.

3.6. Model information not paper

A common mistake made by analysts is to map the flow of paper around the business as opposed to the flow of information.

Diagram correctly showing the flow of information between Functions

The above diagram is correct as it shows the flow of the information that is needed to carry out the Function "Bill the Customer".

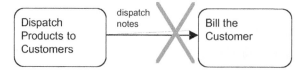

Diagram wrongly showing the flow of paper as opposed to the flow of information

The above diagram is wrong as it shows the flow of paper – "dispatch notes" - and not of the information needed by the Function "Bill the Customer".

The main reason this is wrong is that paper reports can carry several (often many) different pieces of information and just showing the name of the piece of paper or report does not show us what information is needed by the receiving Function.

Some analysts compound the problem of paper flow further as shown below.

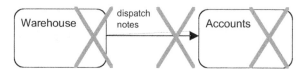

Diagram showing the flow of paper between departments

The above diagram is **NOT** an Information Flow Diagram.

Not only is it incorrect because it shows the flow of paper as opposed to the flow of information, but the boxes represent **Departments** in the business as opposed to **Business Functions** – remember a **department is not a Function!!** (another mistake made by analysts and businesspeople alike).

Sometimes it is desirable to show the flow of paper around the business to demonstrate a specific point, for example, the proliferation of paper. The proper technique for doing this is described in Section 0.

3.7. Multiple Information Flows

When more than one piece of information flows from one Function to another this is shown by a **single** arrow but with **multiple** labels – one for each major piece of information flowing – each separated by commas.

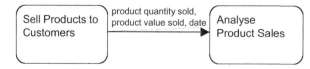

Multiple pieces of information flowing from one Function to another

3.8. Create/Transform Rule (1)

A basic definition of a Function is that it must either **create** or **transform** information. This is an essential rule to know when building and quality checking IFDs.

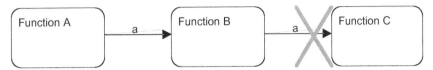

The same information should not flow into and out of a Function

Because of the Create/Transform Rule the same information cannot flow **into** and **out of** a Function.

In the diagram above information flow 'a' goes into Function B and out the other side. This is an error. Information cannot flow through a Function without being transformed – or it is not a Function.

If both Function B and Function C require the information 'a' then the diagram should be drawn as below:

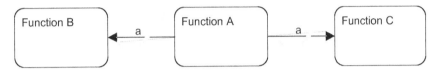

Information should be shown going directly from source to where it is required

Here the Information Flow 'a' is shown coming from Function A, which is source. An Information Flow should always be shown emerging from the Function that creates it. It can never pass through another Function unchanged.

This is one of the basic quality checks that ought to be made on all Information Flow Diagrams.

3.9. Create/Transform Rule (2)

The following diagram also breaks the Create/Transform rule as Function C is receiving information but is not creating or transforming any information - as there is no Information Flow out of it.

All Functions must have information flowing out (different to that flowing in)

A Function must always create or transform information. It must, therefore, always have an output.

If it does not have an output, it is not a Function!

This is another basic quality check to make on an Information Flow Diagram.

3.10. Create/Transform Rule (3)

The error of passing information unchanged through a Function can be compounded by analysts when they incorrectly map **'distribution mechanisms'** within the business as **Functions**.

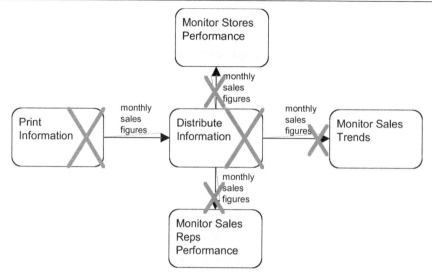

A distribution "department" mistaken for a Function

The above diagram was used to map the activities of the Print Room and Post Room in a Brewery. The analysts invented the 'Functions' "Print Information" and "Distribute Information" to make the diagram work but these are mechanisms and not real Functions!

> For an explanation of the difference between Functions and mechanisms, get our book,
> **IMM Requirements Gathering and Business Function Modeling,**
> available from Amazon and Kindle in both Paperback and eBook format.
> Simply search for "integrated modeling method".

What is happening in the above diagram is that the Monthly Sales Report is produced by the Print Room and given to the Post Room for distribution. The diagram shows the **flow of paper**. This actually hides the **true flow of information**, which is shown below.

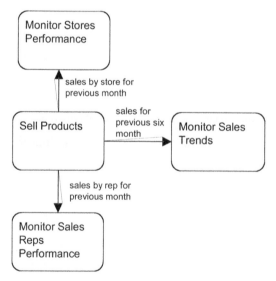

The true flow of information

The above diagram solves the problem and shows the true flow of information.

Using the basic quality checks of not showing paper flow and ensuring that the Create/Transform rule is obeyed will help you avoid the errors in the original diagram.

4.   Defining Information Flows

The definition for an information flow should contain all the following elements.

Element	Description
Name	**This is mandatory**. Every information flow must have a name, or it is a meaningless arrow. The name should consist of a short phrase that describes the essence of the information flow without defining its contents e.g., 'monthly sales figures'. The label is always written in lowercase and placed next to the arrow representing the information flow on the IFD.
Description	This expands on the name. Suppose the label was 'monthly sales figures', the description for this might be: "Monetary value of the sales of all products for the preceding calendar month". This Description would not appear on the IFD but would appear in supporting documentation or in a CASE Tool.
Data Elements	This describes the elements of data that make up the information flow. Attributes of entities are prefixed with the entity name for example: PRODUCT.Code PRODUCT.Name Derived elements are prefixed with 'Derived', for example: DERIVED.Total Product Value Each derived element may need to have a description to unambiguously describe what it is, for example: "The total of all sales values for a product in the preceding calendar month". The listing of the data elements would not appear on the IFD but would appear in supporting documentation or in a CASE Tool.

**For more information on Entities and Attributes, get our book,
IMM Business Requirements Gathering and Data Architecture Modeling,
available from Amazon and Kindle in both Paperback and eBook format.
Simply search for "integrated modeling method".**

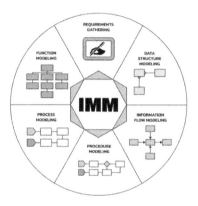

5. Information Flow Modeling Workshops

IFDs are built during Information Flow modeling workshops.

The interviewees at these workshops should be one or two (no more) key people from the business who know the information needs of the Functions being modelled.

The starting point for modeling Information Flows is the Function Catalogue. Information Flows are modelled for Functions at the bottom level of the Function Catalogue. Ideally these should be Elementary Business Functions (EBF's). If they are not, the Information Flow modeling workshop is a good point to break them down to that level.

> **For full descriptions of the Function Catalogue, Functions and Elementary Business Functions (EBF's)**
> **get our book, IMM Requirements Gathering and Business Function Modeling,**
> **available from Amazon and Kindle in both Paperback and eBook format.**
> **Simply search for "integrated modeling method".**

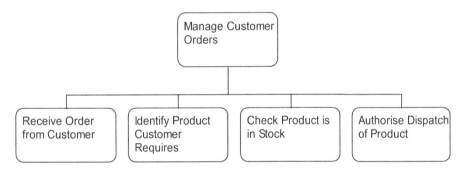

Example of a small part of a Function Catalogue

Prior to the workshop the interviewees should be sent a diagram of that part of the Function Catalogue holding the Functions for which the Information Flows need to be modelled. This will show where the Functions fit into the overall business. This diagram will act as the starting point for the modeling workshop. The Function Catalogue should be displayed on a wall of the room in which the workshop is being held.

The first Function for which the Information Flows are to be mapped should be drawn in the middle of a whiteboard – this is the Focal Function. A larger square (not too large) should be drawn around the focal Function – this is the focal box (see Section 3.5 for rules on the focal box).

The interviewees should then be asked the following question:

> "You are the business expert(s) carrying out this Function. What information do you need in order to do so and where does this information come from?"

The 'where' must be expressed either as another Function or as an External Entity.

If the interviewees do not know which Function creates the information and can only give an answer such as "we get it from the Accounts Department" the analyst must think of a suitable Function that would create the information in question.

For example, If the required information was "product sales for the month", then a likely Function to create this would be "Sell Products". This Function should be added to the Information Flow Diagram with an arrow labelled "product sales for the month" coming from it and going to the Focal Function.

The text "To be Verified as Source" should be written alongside this Function to remind the analysts that the source needs to be verified.

The Function Catalogue needs to be checked to see if the Function "Sell Products" already exists on it. If not, it will need to be added. In this way the Function Catalogue is dynamically updated as part of information flow modeling activities.

When you have modelled all the Information Flows required to do the Focal Function you should then ask the question:

> "What information does this (the focal) Function create and where does it go?"

Once again the 'where' must be another Function or an External Entity.

If the interviewees do not know to what Function the created information goes it will not be so easy for the analysts to imagine what that Function might be.

If the interviewees only know the department to which the information flows, then asking the question "What is it used for there?" might help to establish the Function. If the interviewees only know the people to whom the information is given, then asking the question "What do they do with it?" might also help.

If they can answer none of these questions, then a Function should be added to the diagram with the name "Dummy Function" and the information flow shown going to this. The text "To Be Verified" should be placed next to the dummy Function to highlight it and prevent it remaining unverified. The arrow going from the Focal Function to the Dummy Function will be labelled with the information that is created by the Focal Function.

The final Information Flow Diagram should have all such dummy Functions converted to valid Functions.

6.   Verifying Information Flow at the Receiving Function

Information ought never to be thought of as being 'pushed' from one Function to the next. The Function that needs the information should be thought of as 'pulling' it from the Functions that create it, as and when it is needed.

For this reason, it is essential always to check with those people in the business that carry out the Function receiving information that they really do require the information that is being sent to them.

When asked "do you need this information?" they will very often answer "No, we are sent it all the time, but we never use it".

In this case the information flow should be removed from the diagram.

Another response that is common is "Oh Yes! They send us that report every month, but we never use it. We get the information we need from another report."

This response seems to suggest that the receiving Function does not require the information in question, but all that is really telling us is that the *report* in question is not used as the source of the information, but that a different report is used. But as we learned in Section 3.6, we must model the flow of information and not the flow of paper. So, the **information MUST** be shown coming from the Function that created it. (see also the Single Source Rule below).

This is another example where the business thinks about (and describes) the flow of documents (in this case reports) as opposed to the flow of information. It is important for analysts not to fall into the same trap.

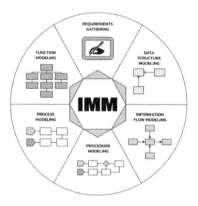

7.   The Single Source Rule

One of the fundamental rules for Information Flow modeling is the Single Source Rule for information, which is:

> **The Single Source Rule**
> **Any discrete, unique piece of information can only ever have one Business Function as its source. The information that a Business Function creates helps to uniquely identify the Business Function itself, therefore, if two Business Functions create the same piece of information then they are in fact the same Business Function – not two!**

This is a very powerful rule for validating Information Flow Diagrams because it tells us that if the same item of information seems to be flowing from two different sources, then there is an error.

In such circumstances either the items of information are in essence different (they have been wrongly given the same name) or the Functions from which they come are the same (but have wrongly been given names that make them seem different).

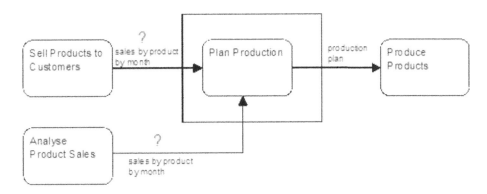

Diagram showing same information flow coming from two different sources

In the above diagram the information flow 'sales by product by month' is shown coming from two different sources. Because we know the Single Source Rule, we know that there is a mistake here.

If we look at the contents of both information flows, we will see that they are different.

The information flow coming from "Sell Products to Customers" would be better named "product sales". This would probably consist of the data items 'product', 'quantity', 'date'.

The information flow coming from "Analyze Product Sales" is probably properly named "sales by product by month" because this Function will have taken the raw sales information from the Function "Sell Products to Customers" (this flow is not shown on the diagram as it is outside the focal box) and totaled it by product for each month. This is the type of information needed to plan production. The raw sales data from "Sell Products to Customers" would be of little use, as it has not been analyzed, and ought to be removed from the diagram.

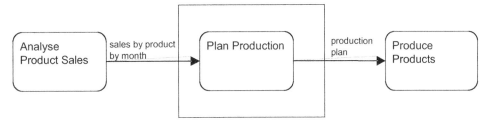

Amended diagram with duplicate information flow removed

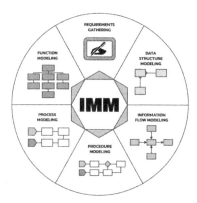

8.   Modeling Flow of paper

If the business needs to model the flow of documents (such as reports) around the business this can easily be achieved by adding the documents to Information Flow Diagrams.

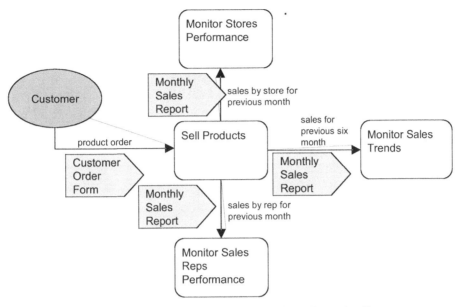

Diagram showing flow of documents added to information flows
(The focal box has been omitted for clarity)

The diagram above demonstrates how to show the flow of paper between Functions. A block arrow is placed next to the information flow between the Functions and the name of the document or report that contains the information is written inside the block arrow.

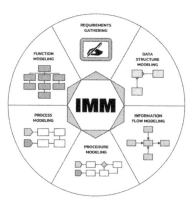

9.   Information Overload

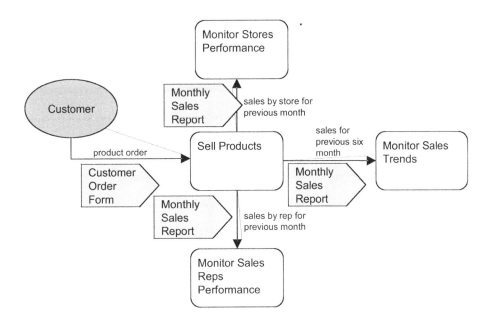

In the previous diagram, shown above, three different Information Flows to three different Functions are achieved using one report. Initially this might seem to be very efficient as only one report is needed.

This situation hides the curse of most businesses in that managers receive far more (and inappropriate) information than they need, and they must delve through reports to find what is relevant to them. In essence most reports hold a lot of unwanted information.

In the diagram above the person doing the Function "Monitor Sales Representatives' Performance" only needs the information 'sales value by representative' but gets all the information in the report.

The same happens with the person doing the Function "Monitor Stores' Performance" who only needs the information 'sales value by store'. Likewise with the Function "Analyze Product Sales".

This is the major reason why analysts should **never ask the business** the question **"what reports do you want?"**.

It is the job of the **analyst** to establish the **information** that is needed to carry out the Function. It is the job of **system designers** to decide (in consultation with the business) the **best method** of getting that information to them. This may be in report form, or graph form. It may be in paper form or on a computer screen.

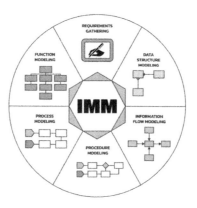

10. Information Flow vs Process

One of the major errors made by analysts is to use Information Flow Diagrams in place of Process Diagrams. They incorrectly assume that the flow of information between Functions equates to the flow of control in a process model.

This is a major error and should be avoided at all costs. The following subsections explain the problem and the solution.

10.1. Precedence

When a business wishes to know the precise order in which Functions are carried out, then the model to use is a **Process Model**.

Precedence in a Process Model

In a Process Model an arrow going from one Function to another (as shown above) tells us two things:

- Function B cannot begin until Function A is complete.
- Function B can begin at any time convenient to the business, after Function A has been completed.

In other words, Function A **'precedes'** Function B – this is '**precedence'**.

> Because Function A occurs before Function B it is placed to the left of Function B and the overall flow of the process is from left to right. (Process flow could also be shown going from top to bottom but that is unusual and is not the standard in IMM). The arrow indicates flow of **control** through the process from one Function to the next.

On an Information Flow Diagram, the arrow going from one Function to another indicates the flow of Information and **NOT** the flow of control.

The ideal layout of an Information Flow Diagram is to set the focal Function in the center of the diagram with all the information it requires flowing in and all the information it creates flowing out, from and to other Functions set radially around it. There are two main reasons for this:

1. It brings into focus the focal Function and all the Functions with which it exchanges information.
2. It prevents an Information Flow Diagram being thought of as a process.

10.2. Inferring Precedence (1)

The following diagram shows the flow of information between Functions.

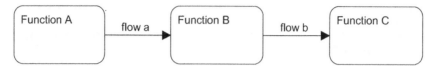

Diagram showing flow of information

When looking at the above diagram many analysts make the mistake of assuming that it equates to a process and infer precedence in the following way:

- If Function B needs information flow 'a' then Function A must occur **before** Function B.
- In Function C needs information flow 'b' then Function B must occur **before** Function C.

However, in reality this may be very different from the true way in which the Functions occur in a defined process.

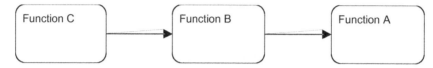

Diagram showing flow of control

From a **process** point of view what might happen is that Function C gets triggered by a business event. It then triggers Function B in order to get the information it requires. Function B in turn triggers Function A to get the information it requires. This is the **EXACT OPPOSITE** of that inferred from looking at the Information Flow Diagram!!

The basic message here is that **Information Flow Diagrams are not, and ought to never be thought of or used as, Process Models!!!**

10.3. Inferring Precedence (2)

The following set of diagrams demonstrates another way in which analysts confuse information flow and process flow.

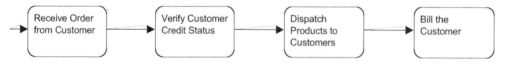

Diagram showing flow of control

The above diagram shows the flow of control through the process. Does this equate to the flow of information? Bad analysts would make the mistake of thinking so and they would show 'order details' flowing into the first Function and then through each Function in turn as in the following diagram.

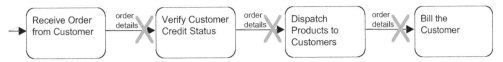

Diagram incorrectly showing flow of information equating to flow of control

The above diagram is incorrect because:

- It breaks the Create / Transform rule that tells us that a Function always creates or transforms information and cannot pass information through unchanged.
- It makes the mistakes on inferring precedence as described in Section 10.2 above.

The following diagram shows the true flow of information between the Functions in question.

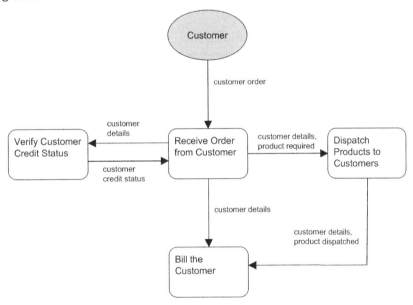

IFD showing the true flow of information

In the above diagram the Information Flow from "Dispatch Products to Customers" to "Bill the Customer" is shown for completeness. This flow, being outside the focal box would not normally need to be shown.

In the following diagram we superimpose the flow of information on the process diagram. The information flows are shown as red arrows.

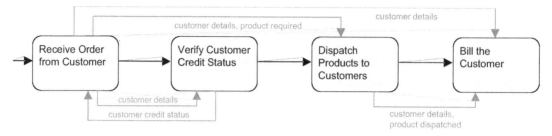

Diagram showing information flow superimposed on process flow

The above diagram shows the essential difference between the flow of control and the flow of information.

This once again reinforces the basic message: **Information Flow Diagrams are not, and ought to never be thought of or used as Process Models!**

**For a full and detailed descriptions of Process Modeling
get our book, IMM Process Modeling,
available from Amazon and Kindle in both Paperback and eBook format.
Simply search for "integrated modeling method".**

---

11. Exercise: IFD Errors

The diagram below shows an Information Flow Diagram that has been modelled without following the rules that have been described in this book. Because of this, it contains SIX modeling errors.

For this exercise you have to examine this Information Flow Diagram and:

- Identify and highlight the six errors.

- Explain why they are errors.

- Correct the errors.

- Explain why your actions have corrected the errors.

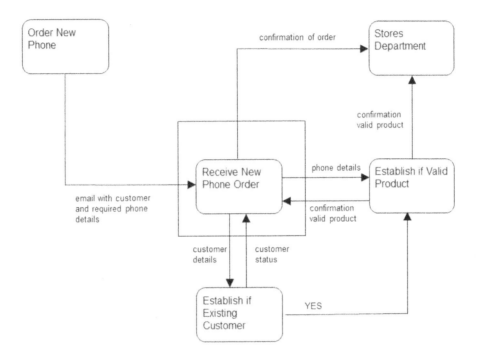

Information Flow Diagram with Five Errors

The solutions to this exercise can be found In Section 15

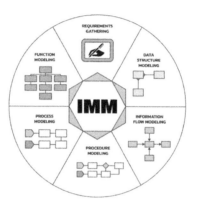

12. IFD's Versus DFD's

In IMM, Information Flow Diagrams (IFD's) are used to represent the flow of information around a business and between the business and the outside world.

Some analysts may have previously used Data Flow Diagrams (DFD's) and, noting the similarities with IFD's think that they are both the same thing. **They are not!** IFD's, although similar to DFD's have several essential differences that make them more robust and less prone to error.

Below is a list of the facets of DFD's that are not used in Information Flow Modeling in IMM together with the reasons why these elements are unsafe to use in Business Modeling.

Data Store	These are symbols that can be placed on DFD's to represent places where data is stored, either in the current business environment or in a future planned computer system.
	This is an unsafe practice as it breaks one of the fundamental rules of business analysis that says that all business analysis and modeling should be done independently of current or future 'systems' or design thinking.
Logical and Physical Perspectives	In methods that employed DFD's as their main modeling technique (such as SSADM) there were many different 'views' of the world that a DFD could represent. These included:

	Current Physical	This meant a view of how the business is currently carried out but sadly included a 'warts and all' approach that entailed modeling even the most incorrect practices of the business in full detail!! A practice that takes considerable time and is of no value.
	Current Logical	The term 'logical' was meant to be the opposite of 'physical'. This 'view' is close to how business modeling should be done but was flawed because it was based on the 'current physical' view with its 'warts and all'.
	Future Logical	This 'view' is closest to how business modeling should be done but is flawed because it tried to 'imagine' **HOW** the business would operate in the future and so modelled mechanisms as opposed to Business Functions.
	Future Physical	This is not really a business modeling technique at all but really a 'design' approach to model future 'procedures'.

Diagram Decomposition	Those methods that use DFD's also tend to use decomposition (breaking down into more detail) of these diagrams. **This is a practice to be avoided at all costs,** as it is extremely cumbersome, prone to error, adds no value and results in 3 to 5 times more diagrams being drawn than are necessary. In IMM all decomposition is done using the Function Catalogue, where it is easy to do and where it adds value.
Flow Levelling	This is a cumbersome practice resulting from decomposing DFD's in which the data flows have themselves to be broken down into more and more detail. It is another practice to be avoided at all costs and is not necessary in IMM.

In IMM the primary modeling technique is Business Function Modeling. This is used to build the Function Catalogue and all other models are built using the Functions from the bottom level of the catalogue.

Information Flow Modeling is a secondary modeling technique in IMM and is only used when it is necessary to understand and model how information flows around the business.

We strongly recommend that you become fully familiar with all the facets of Business Function Modeling before you begin using any of the secondary modeling methods. If you do, you will find that your models will be far more rigorous, yet less complicated. Your productivity will also be much higher as you will be able to get it right first time, every time.

> **For full descriptions of Business Function, Business Functions, and Elementary Business Functions (EBF's) read our book, IMM Requirements Gathering and Business Function Modeling, available from Amazon and Kindle in both Paperback and eBook format.**
> **Simply search for "integrated modeling method".**

13. About the Authors

Discover the works of John Owens and Pam Walton, acclaimed thought leaders, speakers, writers, consultants, and mentors. With an impressive array of expertise, they are revolutionizing the world of Business Architecture Modeling. Renowned worldwide for their innovative approaches, John and Pam have spearheaded projects in a diverse range of industries spanning the globe. Their international reputation as highly skilled specialists precedes them, with a successful track record in the UK, Ireland, Europe, Australia, and New Zealand.

Their unique ability to train, coach, and mentor individuals, regardless of technical background, sets them apart. Through their guidance, both technical and non-technical professionals gain the skills to become highly competent analysts and business architects.

As the creators of IMM, the Integrated Modelling Method, they have crafted a series of five groundbreaking books on creating Business Architectures for Enterprises of all types and sizes, that are globally recognized. These books cover the topics of Requirements Gathering, Function Architecture Modeling, Data Architecture Modeling, Business Process Modeling, Business Procedure Modeling, and Information Flow Modeling.

Starting April 2023, their comprehensive collection of IMM books will be available worldwide. Immerse yourself in their powerful insights, whether you prefer the convenience of an eBook from Kindle or the tangible experience of a paperback from Amazon. Stay tuned for exact publishing dates.

For more information, simply reach out via email at support@integrated-modeling.com. Prepare to embark on a transformative journey with John Owens and Pam Walton, where proficiency and success are within your grasp.

14. Please Leave a Positive Review

We would love to know about your experience of reading this book.

If you had a **POSITIVE EXPERIENCE** with the book, then please share this with others by leaving a **POSITIVE REVIEW** on Kindle or Amazon.

If you found anything in it that you think we could improve, then please tell us about by sending an email to:

support@integrated-modeling-method.com

We would love to hear from you.

Thank you

Pam & John

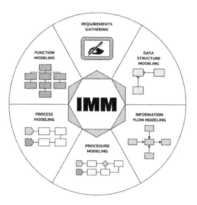

15. Solutions to Exercise

In this Section we will identify, explain, and resolve the errors in the Information Flow Diagram (IFD) from the Exercise: IFD Errors on page 29. In total there are 6 errors.

15.1. Error 1

There is a symbol for a Business Function on the top left of this Information Flow Diagram (IFD) with the name "Order New Phone", which is an action carried out by a Customer. To show this as a Business Function is incorrect because any activity done outside of the Enterprise is **NEVER** a Business Function.

The standard on IFDs is that any 'entity' outside of the Enterprise that sends information to, or receives information from, the Enterprise, is shown as an External Entity.

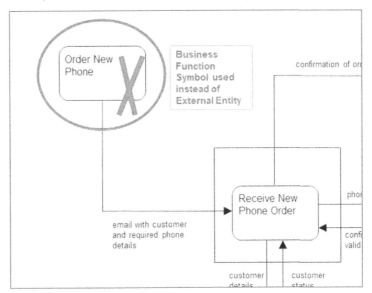

So, the Business Function "Order New Phone" is replaced with an External Entity named "Customer".

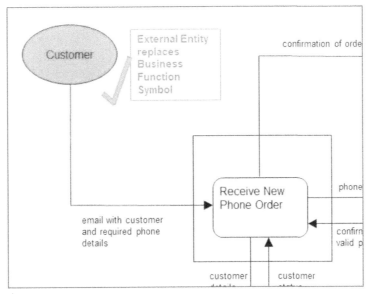

Error 1 is now resolved.

15.2. Error 2

The second error on this IFD is that it models the flow of paper as opposed to the flow of information when showing the flow of a document from Customer to the Business Function "Receive New Phone Order".

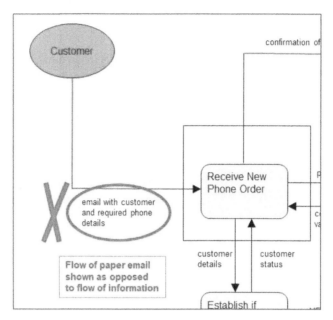

Information Flow Diagram Error 2

We need to replace the flow of paper with the flow of the **RELEVANT I**nformation contained in the email.

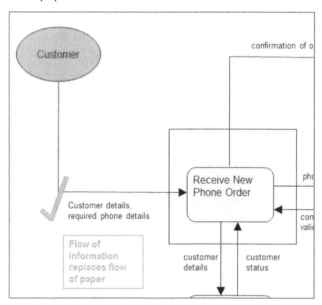

Error 1 Resolved

In this example, the difference might seem trivial, but it is vital for IFD integrity to only show the information that is essential to carry out the Focal Business Function. The main reason for this is that the pieces of paper that flow around an Enterprise often contain lots of information that is not needed by an individual Business Function.

Error 2 is now resolved.

15.3. Errors 3 and 4

The next error is where the arrow going from "Establish if Existing Customer" to "Establish if Valid Product" is labeled "YES". This is the structure of a *conditional branch*, which is valid on a Business Process Model but **NOT** on an IFD. All lines on IFDs show flow of **INFORMATION**, not flow of control.

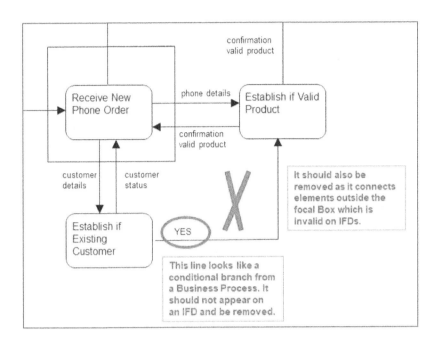

This same arrow also represents another error as it connects two objects *outside* the focal box, which is an invalid structure on an IFD.

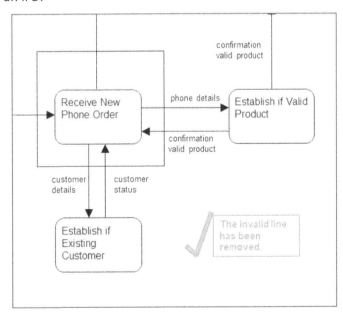

This diagram shows that the offending arrow has been removed and resolved Errors 3 and 4.

15.4. Error 5

The next error is the line going from "Establish if Valid Product" to "Stores Department". Although this line represents a valid flow of information from the "Establish if Valid Product" to the "Stores Department" it ought not be shown on the IFD as it connects elements outside of the Focal Box.

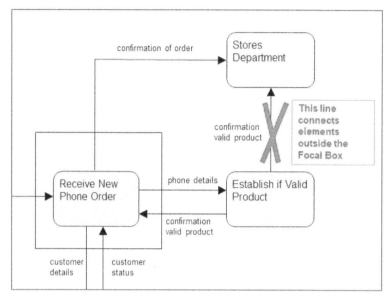

The incorrect line is removed.

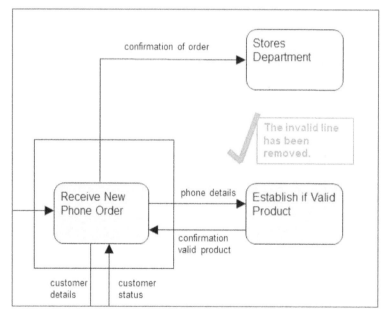

Error 5 is now resolved.

15.5. Error 6

The final error in this IFD is the Business Function symbol at the top right, labelled "Stores Department ".

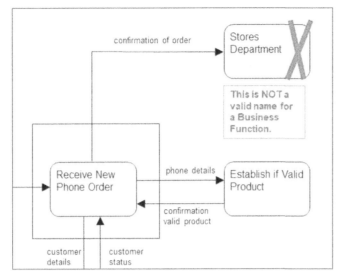

Although the symbol is a Business Function, it has the name "Stores Department", which is not a valid name for a Business Function.

There are two valid ways to resolve this modeling problem.

- **Option 1:** Replace the Business Function with an External Entity labelled "Stores Department".
- **Option 2**: Give the Business Function an appropriate name, for example, "Prepare Product for Dispatch".

Solution 6 Option 1

This is the option to use if the Stores Department lies outside the "Management Horizon" of the Management Team for the Focal Business Function. (**See Definition for Management Horizon** below).

When this is case, the Management Team for the Focal Business Function will have no knowledge of what Business Functions in the Stores Department receive or send information to the Focal Business Function.

Because of this, the Stores Department is shown as an External Entity on the IFD, as in the diagram on the right.

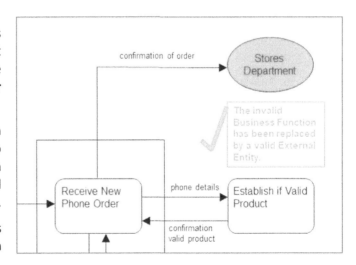

Solution 6 Option 2

In this option, the Stores Department lies within the Management Horizon for the Management Team for the Focal Business Function.

When this is the case, the Management Team knows precisely what Business Function in the Stores Department receives the Information Flow "Confirmation of Order" from the Business Function "Receive New Phone Order".

Because of this, the Business Function on the IFD is given the correct name of "Prepare Product for Dispatch"

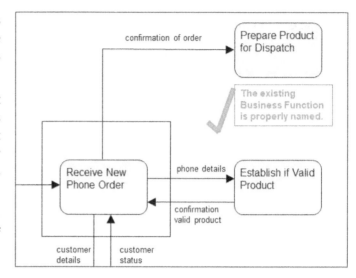

15.6. Definition for Management Horizon

The term "Management Horizon" refers to those Business Functions over which the owners of the Focal Business Function on an IFD have management control.

The concept of the Management Horizon is important as there is a simple rule when doing Information Flow Modeling – 'you can only show Business Functions on an IFD if they lie within your Management Horizon'.

When objects outside the Management Horizon need to appear on an IFD then they are shown as External Entities.

16. Glossary

This glossary contains definitions for all the elements of the **Business Architecture Models** of IMM, listed alphabetically. These models are Business Function Models, Business Process Models, Data Architecture Models, Business Procedure Models, Information Flow Models.

Where a definition contains a term that is defined elsewhere in the glossary it appears in **bold italic**.

Term	Description
Alphanumeric	This is the term used to denote that a **Data Entity Attribute** can contain all standard alphabetic and numeric characters. Although alphanumeric attributes can contain numeric characters they should **NOT** be thought of as numbers to be mathematically manipulated. If such manipulation is required, then the attribute should be defined as **numeric**.
Analysis and Extraction	This is the activity of analyzing all the materials collected during the **Requirements Gathering** stage of a **Business Improvement Project** and identifying and extracting **Business Functions** or **Data Entities** from them.
Analysis Stage	This is the stage of a **Business Improvement Project**, usually one to build a new software system, where the Enterprise is analyzed and modeled. The purpose of this analysis and modeling is to enable a system to be designed, built, and implemented that will support the effective execution of the **Business Functions** of the **Enterprise**.
AND Connector	This is where two or more flows in a **Business Process** from separate **Process Steps** (**Business Functions**) are merged into one flow before entering another **Process Step**.
Atomic Business Function	A **Business Function** at the bottom level of a **Business Function Hierarchy**. It is a Business Function with no **Child Business Functions**.
Attribute	A term commonly used to refer to **Data Entity Attributes**.
Business Aim	Some goal that a business wishes to achieve, for example, "Become the largest supplier of accountancy software in the UK". See also **Business Objective**.
Business Architecture Model	The term used to refer to a set of models built to represent a particular aspect of the Enterprise activities of an Enterprise. In IMM these models include **Business Function Model**, **Business Process Model**, **Business Procedure Model**, **Data Architecture Model**, and **Information Flow Model**.
Business Champion	A person from within the Enterprise who plays an active part in a business improvement or systems development project whose major role is to "champion" the improvement within the Enterprise.
Business Function	A **Business Function** - also called a Function - is an activity or set of activities that a business must perform to meet its **Business Aims** and **Business Objectives** and continue in existence.
Business Function Decomposition	This is the term used to describe splitting **Business Functions** on the **Business Function Hierarchy** into lower-level **Business Functions**.

Term	Description
Business Function Description	A written description, in plain English, of what a **Business Function** is meant to do.
Business Function Hierarchy	The structuring of **Business Functions** into a hierarchical format with a **Root Business Function** at the top, **Grouping Business Functions** below that and **Atomic Business Functions** or **Elementary Business Functions** at the bottom.
Business Function Logic	A formal structured definition of what a **Business Function** does, using structured English, flowcharts, formulae, tables, etc. This would be an expansion of the **Business Function Description**.
Business Function Name	A short unique, succinct name for a **Business Function** that encapsulates the objective of that **Business Function**.
Business Function Objective	A concise statement of the purpose of a **Business Function**, i.e., what it is meant to achieve.
Business Improvement Project	Any project that is carried out with the intention of improving the performance of some aspect of an **Enterprise**. This improvement could take several forms, such as, structure, communications, conditions, systems, technology, etc..
Business Objective	A measurable **Business Aim**. For example, if the **Business Aim** for the **Enterprise** was "Become the largest supplier of accountancy software in the UK", then making this measurable by adding, say, "within three years" would change it to a **Business Objective**. The acronym **SMART** is a useful way to ensure that a **Business Objective** is properly and fully defined. Each objective should be **S**pecific, **M**easurable, **A**chievable, **R**ealistic and **T**rackable

Term	Description
Business Procedure	A *Business Procedure* is a set of steps to follow to perform a *Business Function* or a *Business Process* in line with current business practices, standards, and policies. **Example:** The procedure to follow to perform the *Business Function* "Charge Customers for Products and Services Supplied" might be as follows: • Collect signed delivery notes from Distribution Supervisor • Check that delivery date is in the current financial month, if it is not, then file the delivery note in the "Pending" tray • Create a new invoice in the invoicing system • Enter details of the goods and services supplied • Enter any extraordinary charges or rebates (such as rebates for pallets) • "Post" invoice to the ledger using F10 key • Stamp delivery note as "processed" adding your initials and the date • File delivery notes • Print invoices • Sort invoices by customer • Post (send) invoice to customer Both businesspeople, and analysts often mistake *Business Procedures* for *Business Processes*.
Business Process	A *Business Process* – also commonly called a process – describes the order of execution of *Business Functions* in response to a specific *trigger* in order to achieve a *Preferred* or *Non-Preferred Outcome*.
Business Process Description	A description, in plain English, of what a Business Process does, what it includes and what it excludes. It is an expansion of the *Process Objective*.
Business Process Diagram	A diagram visually depicting a *Business Process*.
Business Process Flow	A term that refers to the order in which *Business Functions* are carried out in a *Business Process*.
Business Process Name	A unique name for a *Business Process* that succinctly encapsulates the objective of the Business Process.
Business Process Objective	A definition of what a *Business Process* is intended to achieve. This objective should align to the *Preferred Outcome* for the *Business Process*.
Business Process Step	A single step in a *Business Process*. Business Process steps are ALWAYS *Business Functions* taken from the bottom level of the *Business Function Hierarchy*, being either *Atomic Business Functions* or *Elementary Business Functions*.

Term	Description
Business Requirements	A term commonly used to refer to what a business needs or requires a ***Business Improvement Project*** to achieve. The term is too general to be useful and needs to be stated in quite specific terms, such as, "Business Functions to be supported", "performance requirements", "security needs", etc.
Business Sponsor	A person from within the ***Enterprise*** (usually an Executive or Senior Manager) who provides the budget and political drive to bring about the successful execution of a ***Business Improvement Project***.
Candidate Business Function	Any phrase found when analyzing gathered ***Business Requirements,*** that <u>contains a verb</u> that represents an action or activity carried out as part of the business operation of an ***Enterprise***. All such verb phrases are 'potential' or ***Candidate Business Functions***.
Candidate Data Entity	Any noun contained in an ***interview transcript***, ***Business Function*** name or flow on an ***Information Flow Diagram*** is a ***candidate data entity*** and should be included in the list of ***Candidate Data Entities*** that is built as part of the ***Data Extraction Stage*** of ***Data Architecture Modeling***. When consolidated, the items in this list will turn out to be: • ***True data entities*** • ***Attributes*** of entities • ***Occurrences*** of entities • ***Subtypes*** of entities • ***Synonyms*** for entities
CASE Tool	**CASE** stands for "Computer Aided Systems Engineering". The term "CASE Tool" refers to a computer application which is designed to aid in the analysis and modeling of ***Enterprises*** and the design and construction of systems to support these operations of these ***Enterprises***.
Child Business Function	Any ***Business Function*** in a ***Business Function Hierarchy*** grouped under a ***Grouping Business Function***. All ***Grouping Business Functions*** can also be referred to as a ***Parent Business Functions*** because they have "children".
Consolidated List of Business Functions	The final list of ***Candidate Business Functions*** after all ***Mechanisms*** and duplications have been removed.
Critical Success Factor	A ***Critical Success Factor (CSF)*** is something that must occur in a project or in a business activity for it to be deemed successful. For example: • A ***CSF*** for a business activity might be that the response time to customer queries is reduced from 15 minutes to 5 minutes within three months. • A ***CSF*** for a project might be that the old accounting system can be switched off by the end of the financial year.

Term	Description
Data	A value in a particular format is called a datum. However, this singular form is now seldom used, having been superseded with the more familiar plural form, **Data**. Examples of items of data are: **Datum** **Description** 1 Integer to one significant figure. red Character string, three characters in length, lower case 3.9 Number with two significant digits and one place of decimals. 22 Oct 22 Date with numeric day number, first three characters of the month name (initial letter capitalized) and last two digits of the year.
Data Architecture Model	The full definition of the **data entities** and the structure they require to provide an **Enterprise** with the **Information** it requires to effectively execute its **Business Functions**. A complete **Data Architecture Model** will include: • A **Data Structure Diagram** • **Data Entity** definitions, volumes, synonyms, etc. • **Data Attribute** definitions and formats. • **Relationship** definitions • **Data Entity** and **Attribute** usage by **Business Functions, Business Departments** and **Automated Systems.**
Data Entity	A data entity, normally called an "entity", is anything (whether real or abstract) of significance to the Enterprise about which information must be known or held to support the **Business Functions**. Typical entities for a company might be "Customer", "Product", "Sales Transaction". Data is always either created or transformed by **Business Functions**. **Data is ONLY of SIGNIFICANCE to an Enterprise if it can be turned into INFORMATION that supports the execution of Business Functions.**
Data Entity Attribute	**Data Entity Attributes** describe, classify, qualify, or quantify **Data Entities**. Every **Data Entity Attribute** has a name and a **format**, for example: • Age: Number (2) • Description: Character (75) • Name: Character (25) • Weight: Number (4,2) **Data Entity Attributes** are commonly referred to simply as **Attributes**.

Term	Description
Data Extraction Process	The process of identifying and extracting **Candidate Data Entities** from **interview transcripts**, **Business Functions**, or **Information Flow Diagrams** as these are all **Candidate Data Entities.**
Data Flow Diagram	A diagram used in traditional business analysis, normally referred to as a **DFD**, showing the flow of data between **Business Functions**, **external entities**, and **data stores**. DFD's have been superseded in IMM by **information flow diagrams**.
Data Format	This refers to the format in which data is held by **Data Entity Attributes**. For example, the entity **Part** might have the following attributes and formats:
	Attribute **Format**
	Name Alphanumeric 35 characters in length – the abbreviation for this would be "Char (35)".
	Weight Number with four significant digits and two places of decimals – abbreviated to Num (4,2).
Data Store	A symbol on a **Data Flow Diagram (DFD)** representing an existing or planned means for storing **data**, usually a **Database**. **DFDs** are not used in IMM as they have many structural flaws that break the rules of good analysis.
Data Structure	A description of all the **Data Entities** in an **Enterprise** and the **relationships** between them.
Data Structure Diagram	A diagram displaying the **Data Entities** of an **Enterprise** and the relationships between them. A **Data Structure Diagram** is a major component of a **Data Architecture Model**.
Data Type	This refers to the type of **data** that a **Data Entity Attribute** can hold. The main **data types** are **alphanumeric**, **numeric**, **integer** and **date**.
Dependency	A term used (but not in IMM) to describe the association between two **Business Functions** on a **Business Process Diagram**.
Design Stage	This is the stage of a systems development project that follows the analysis stage and precedes the build stage. It is a vital stage in developing quality automated information systems. It is here that the system to be built is specified in physical detail. This specification, or "design", can be checked against the **Business Models** created during the analysis stage to ensure that it will properly support these models before the system is built.
DFD	See **Data Flow Diagram**.
Direct Form	This is the statement of an association between two objects, either in a **Business Process Model** or on a **Data Structure Diagram**, based on the order in which the objects appear. See also **Reverse Form**.

Term	Description
Elementary Business Function	This is a *Business Function* which, once begun, must be completed or, if not completed, must be undone.
	If there is a **VALID** intermediate stage for the *Business Function*, then it is **NOT** Elementary.
	At the end of the analysis stage of a systems development, **ALL** bottom level *Business Functions* on the *Business Function Hierarchy* ought to be *Elementary Business Functions*.
Enterprise	This is a generic name used in IMM to refer to businesses, organizations, local government departments, educational institutes, etc. that need to operate as a structured entity in order achieve some defined objective.
Entity	See *Data Entity*.
Entity Relationship Diagram	A diagram showing *Data Entities* and the relationships between them, normally referred to as an *ERD*. This diagram in IMM is called a *Data Structure Diagram*.
ERD	See *Entity Relationship Diagram*.
Event	A happening of significance to an *Enterprise* to which it must respond. There are two classes of *Event*:
	• **Triggers:** these are events to which the Enterprise must respond by starting up a *Business Function* or a *Business Process*.
	• **Outcomes:** these are events that arise as the result of the completion of a *Business Function* or *Business Process*.
External Entity	This is an element on an *Information Flow Diagram* representing an object outside the Enterprise, for example, Customer, Government, Supplier, to which *Information* flows or from which *Information* is received.
Focal Business Function	A *Business Function*, usually an *Elementary Business Function*, drawn at the center of an *Information Flow Diagram*. All *Data Flows* on the diagram are shown going to or from the *Focal Business Function*.
Function	See *Business Function*.
Grouping Business Function	This is a *Business Function* on a *Business Function Hierarchy* whose purpose it is to group lower-level *Business Functions* in a meaningful way.
Handoff	This is a term used when a business department passes control of a *Business Process* or *Business Procedure* to another department or to a third party outside the *Enterprise*. The term can be used in reverse when the other department or external party passes control back to the original department.
IFD	See *Information Flow Diagram*.
IMM	The *Integrated Modeling Method*.

Term	Description
Information	*Data* on its own has little meaning. For example, K3P3 is a *datum*, but what is it? Is it a cipher in a secret code, a foreign car registration or instructions in a knitting pattern (Knit 3, Purl 3)? Data in a context is Information **Data is ONLY of SIGNIFICANCE if it can be turned into INFORMATION that supports the execution of Business Functions.**
Information Flow Diagram	A diagram showing how *Information* flows from one *Business Function* to another or from a Business Function to a third party outside the E*nterprise*. In IMM all information flows are drawn between *Atomic Business Functions* or between *Elementary Business Functions*, whichever are at the bottom of the *Business Function Model,* at this point in time.
Instance of an Entity	If a business has a *Data Entity* called <u>Employee</u>, real life examples of this *Data Entity* might be the employees Fred Jones, John Thomson, and Karen Donnelly. Such real-life examples are referred to as *instances* or *occurrences* of the *Data Entity* <u>Employee</u>.
Integer	This term is used to denote that a *Data Entity Attribute* is a whole number (no decimal places) that can be mathematically manipulated. The convention allows the size of the integer to be specified as well, for example **Int(6)** denotes that the integer has six significant digits. If the number is required to have decimal places the attribute should be defined as being *numeric*.
Internal Trigger	An *Event* that occurs inside the Enterprise to which it must respond by initiating either a *Business Function* or *Business Process*.
Intersection Entity	A *Data Entity* that resolves a *many to many relationship* between two *Data Entities.*
Interview Transcript	A typed or written copy of what was said at an analysis interview.
Key	A term often incorrectly applied to the *Unique Identifier* of a *Data Entity*. Keys (primary keys, unique keys, foreign keys) are not part of *Business Modeling* but of *Systems Design*. So, this term should **NOT** be used in *Business Modeling*.
Key Performance Indicator	A measure by which a *Business Function* is measured in terms of performing well or badly.
Leaf Business Function	Another name for an *Atomic Business Function*.
Loop, Looping	A *loop* in a *Business Process* is where control is passed back to a *Business Function* that has previously been executed in the *Business Process* for it to be executed again, in order to arrive at a desired state.

Term	Description
Many to Many Relationship	A *relationship* between two *Data Entities* that can have many *occurrences* of each *Data Entity* related to each other.
Mechanism	A *Mechanism* is the means by which a *Business Function* is physically performed.
	For example, the Business Function "Bill Customers for Products and Services Supplied" might be executed by either of the following Mechanisms:
	• Print and post an invoice
	• Electronic Data Interchange (EDI)
	In EDI the computer of the supplier communicates directly with the computer of the customer and delivers an "electronic invoice".
Non-Preferred Outcome	This is a desirable but non-preferred outcome to a *Business Process*. It is where the Enterprise would desire a Business Process to stop if the *Preferred Outcome* cannot be attained.
Numeric	This term is used to denote that a *Data* A*ttribute* is a number that can be mathematically manipulated. The convention allows the size of the number to be specified as well, for example Num (6,2) denotes that the number has six significant digits with two decimal places.
	See also *Integer*.
Occurrence	This refers to an *occurrence* of a *Data Entity*. "John Smith" could be an occurrence of the *Data Entity* Employee; "England" would be an occurrence of the *Data Entity* Country.
	An occurrence of a *Data Entity* is also known as an **Instance** of a *Data Entity*.
Outcome	See *Preferred Outcome* and *Non-Preferred Outcome*.
Parent Business Function	A *Business Function* in a *Business Function hierarchy* that has other *Business Functions* hanging beneath it. The *Business Functions* hanging beneath the parent Business Function are called *Child Business Functions*.
Performance Indicator	See *Key Performance Indicator*
Precedence	A definition of what *Business Functions* must come before (precede) and follow (succeed) another *Business Function* in a *Business Process.*
Preferred Outcome	The objective that a *Business Process* is intended to achieve. If the *preferred outcome* cannot be achieved, then a predefined *non-preferred outcome* should be achieved instead.

Term	Description
Primary Key	The rules for **Relational Databases** state that **ALL** rows in a **table** must have a unique key and that this unique key cannot be null. This unique key is called the **Primary Key**. The term "primary key" or "key" is often **INCORRECTLY** used when referring to the **unique identifier** of a **data entity** and also confused with a **QUACK**.
Process	See **Business Process**.
QUACK	**Q**uick **U**nique **A**lternative **C**ode or **K**ey. A useful short way of referring to something, usually a product, in an **Enterprise**, e.g., PIPS could be the 'Personal Insurance Plan for Students'. **QUACKS** are often mistakenly used as **Unique Identifiers**.
Recursion	Another name for **looping** in a **Business Process**.
Recursive Relationship	When a **Data Entity** in a **Data Structure Diagram** is related to itself the **relationship** is referred to as a **Recursive Relationship**.
Relationship	A formal definition of the association between two **Data Entities**. Relationships are always two way so, if entity A is related to entity B, then entity B is related to entity A.
Repository Based	This is a term used to describe **CASE tools** that are not just diagramming tools but that hold objects in a database for use whenever and wherever required. All good CASE tools are repository based. All repository-based CASE tools are not necessarily good!
Requirements	The term commonly used to refer to "what a business requires" from a **Business Improvement Project**. It is a term that is too vague to be meaningful and ought to be avoided. See **business requirements**.
Requirements Gathering	This refers to a set of activities carried out at the beginning of a **Business Improvement Project** to find out from the Executive and Management of the **Enterprise** exactly what **The Business Improvement Project** is meant to achieve.
Reverse Form	This is the **STATEMENT** of an association between two objects, either in a **Business Process Model** or on a **Data Structure Model**, based on the **reverse** of the order in which the objects appear, emphasizing any constraints in this **reverse** direction. It is a powerful technique for checking the **Direct Form**. For example, if the direct form stated that "A starts after B" then the reverse form would state "B **CANNOT** start until A has finished".
Root Business Function	This is the **Business Function** at the top (paradoxically) of a **Business Function hierarchy**.
Service Level Agreement	This is an agreement made between an **Enterprise**, its customers, or suppliers or between Enterprise departments on the time it should take to carry out specific tasks. It is an agreement between the parties of the "level of service" that one will provide to another. This "level of service" can be defined in terms of time or quality or both.

Term	Description
SLA	See **Service Level Agreement**.
Standard Business Life Cycle	The **Standard Business Life Cycle** says that, to operate properly and efficiently, an **Enterprise** should first **PLAN** what it is going to do, then **PERFORM** what it has planned, and **MONITOR** what it has done against the plan, re-planning to take account of variances. For this reason, all **Business Functions** that an **Enterprise** must perform can be classed as: **Plan:** Define what needs to be done, when it needs to be done and the resources needed to do **Perform:** Do what was planned to be done. **Monitor:** Check that what was done is what was planned and if not take appropriate action. The Standard **Business Life Cycle** is a useful structure to use at the top level of the **Business Function Hierarchy**.
Strategy Stage	The startup stage of a **Business Improvement Project** when all the major requirements for the project will be defined.
Subtype	This is a term used for a **Data Entity** that is like other entities in most respects but different in some significant detail. The "significant detail" might mean having an **attribute** or a **relationship** that is different. An example of sub types would be **Employee** and **Freelancer**. Both are types of <u>Worker</u> but are different in the attributes that would need to be held for both. In this example Worker would be a **Supertype Data Entity** that included <u>Employee</u> and <u>Freelancer</u> as **Subtype Data Entities**.
Supertype	This refers to a **Data Entity** that is subdivided into two or more **Subtypes**. For example, <u>Worker</u> would be a **Supertype Data Entity** if it had **Subtype Data Entities** of <u>Employee</u> and <u>Freelancer</u>.
SWOT Analysis	**SWOT analysis** identifies and defines the <u>S</u>trengths, <u>W</u>eaknesses, <u>O</u>pportunities and <u>T</u>hreats associated with all or part of an **Enterprise**, specific **Business Functions**, departments, or individuals, in fact for any item of significance. Good **SWOT Analysis** is essential to the success of **Business Improvement Projects** because it allows the **Enterprise** to build on strengths, eliminate weaknesses, capitalize on opportunities, be aware of and reduce threats.
Synonym	A **Data Entity** might be known by different names in various parts of the **Enterprise**. For example, Worker might be variously known as Employee, Recruit, Temp, Laborer, etc. If all these labels are in essence the same thing (the "same" meaning that the information that needs to be known about them is the same) then each are **Synonyms**.
Trigger	An **Event** in an **Enterprise** that initiates the execution of a **Business Function** or a **Business Process**.

Term	Description
True Data Entity	During the **Data Extraction** stage of building a **Data Architecture Model**, many **Candidate Data Entities** will be identified and listed. When these have been consolidated and a unique name selected for each one, they change from being **Candidate Data Entities** to being **TRUE Data Entities**, or, simply, **Data Entities**.
Unique Identifier	The elements that make each **occurrence** of a **Data Entity** unique from a business and human perspective. These elements might be one or more **attributes**, one or more **relationships** or a combination of **attributes** and **relationships**.

See also **QUACK**. |
| **User** | A person who uses a computer system. **This is perhaps one of the most misused terms in Business Improvement Projects,** being commonly used to refer to any member of the Enterprise who is not part of the project team. A user or "one of them" as opposed to "one of us". Good analysts avoid this term completely when referring to members of the Enterprise and use terms that are more accurate in that they refer to specific groups of people, for example, executives, department heads, process managers, senior managers, etc. |
| **Workflow** | This is the activity of scheduling, managing, and monitoring the tasks involved in **Business Procedures** in an **Enterprise** to ensure that they deliver in accordance with **SLA**'s, policy, objectives, or any other relevant business measures. |

Made in the USA
Las Vegas, NV
27 September 2024

95860275R00033